TO
MARY, QUEEN OF SCOTS
THIS BOOK IS DEDICATED
WITHOUT HER PERMISSION
BY ONE OF
HER HUMBLE ADMIRERS

SONNETS TO A RED-HAIRED LADY

(By a Gentleman with a Blue Beard)

AND

FAMOUS LOVE AFFAIRS

BY
DON MARQUIS

DRAWINGS
BY
STUART HAY

GARDEN CITY   NEW YORK
DOUBLEDAY, PAGE & COMPANY
1922

"Suzanne, my beard is blue"

CONTENTS

SONNETS TO A RED-HAIRED LADY

Contents

Contents

CONTENTS

FAMOUS LOVE AFFAIRS

LIST OF TEXT ILLUSTRATIONS

SONNETS TO A RED–HAIRED LADY

Sonnets to a Red-Haired Lady

I.

COMET, shake out your locks and let them
 flare
Across the startled heaven of my soul!
Pluck out the hairpins, Sue, and let her roll!
Don't be so stingy with your blooming hair,
But let the whole created cosmos share
The glory of its colour, flashed and swirled
Like nets of sunset flung to mesh a world. . . .
Don't wear it in a little wad up there!

And yet, Suzanne, my comet and my star.
At times restrain those locks a little, too. . . .
My First Wife let her hair go quite too far
In culinary ways. I beaned her, Sue. . . .
She looked so wistful as she passed away.
That dear, lost woman, Sue! Ah, welladay!

1

II.

PLUNGE shaded eyes adown the flaming
     past
And lamp the locks that set the world
     afire:—
O wig that touched off Troy! O Dido's
     pyre,
Where flame was given back to flame at
     last!
O love that lashed Ulysses to the mast
What time the red-head Sirens smote the
     lyre!
O simps that used to simmer and perspire
When Mary Stuart's furnace ran full blast!

My Second Wife would very often say:
"There's nothing—*nothing*—I can do with
     it
Just after it's been washed!" Ah, wella-
     day!
Sometimes I've thought 'twas almost
     wrong to hit
A woman *hard* . . . I mention this to you
Merely in pensive reminiscence, Sue.

III.

OLD Titian loved your sort of fiery mop,
And down his leagues of canvas, crowned
    with flame,
Walks one long pageant of Torchlight
    Dame,
Nor hath Oblivion any traffic cop
To bid that bright procession swerve or
    stop . . .
I've heard your brother call you Burning
    Shame:
Some day I'll bend that poor simp's vital
    frame
Beyond repair! Suzanne, sweet Carrot Top,

When we are wedded, prithee, don't allow
Your idiot relations near our house . . .
My Third Wife's father wagged a silly pow
In all our councils, Susan. Welladay!
They lie in one grave now, my erstwhile
    spouse,
And he, her sire, who gave the bride away.

IV.

A GOLDEN strangeness through the nights is
    shed
When Summer merges into harvest-time,
The white moon ripens to a globe of red
And human blood grows quick for love or
    crime—
That sanguine sphere has swung too close
    to earth
And flushed the lucent dews of dusk with
    wine,
A sudden madness mingles with men's
    mirth
And pagan fancies walk the wild moon-
    shine. . . .

So am I troubled and not wholly sane
To see your red head floating like that
    moon;
The notions melt and spread inside my
    brain
Till I am crazy as the well-known loon. . . .
My Fourth Wife left me with the moon
    that way;
Some say I slew her, Sue! Ah, welladay!

"I canned her, Sue"

V.

Suzanne, I bid you fling aside your comb
And down the wind let stream your burn-
    ing hair!
My soul, perchance, through midnights of
    despair,
May see it, Sultry Kid, and flutter home!
Or is there danger in that flaming
    dome? . . .
Suppose I fluttered moth-like, frying there
Unto a crackling, Susan! . . . would you
    care,
My pink-beaned Venus crowned with
    fiery foam?

My Fifth Wife had a wad of hair herself;
She used to wash and wash and wash the
    stuff;
I canned her, Sue; I put her on the shelf;
I like clean hair, but still, enough's
    enough. . . .
She'd get it dry the radiator way. . . .
How these old griefs return! Ah, welladay!

VI.

MY TORCHLIGHT DAME!   My Frail Incom-
　　parable!
My sunset Afterglow!   My Aureole!
Does your head symbolize your ardent
　　soul?
Then must your spirit sting its earthly
　　shell
As hot as pepper-sauce that's served in hell!
Shake out those billowy flames and let 'em
　　roll
Across the world until the very Pole
Melts into love and steams beneath their
　　spell!

My Sixth Wife, Sue, *would* fuss with her-
　　picide;
I loathe the odor; in the kindliest way
I choked her; she forgave me as she died. . . .
How these old memories throng! Ah,
　　welladay!
I do not wish to cloud our love with gloom,
But, Sue, avoid all unguents and perfume.

"Would fuss with herpicide"

9

"I steer by you."

VII.

I saw some bright flowers swaying in the
park
And thought how like their life your red
locks blow. . . .
My Flame! My Sunrise and mine After-
glow!
My genial Hearthfire blazing through the
dark!
My Gaudy Kid! Upon life's headlands,
stark
And bleak, over the treacherous tides that
flow,
A beacon light your Fiery Bean doth
throw. . . .
I steer by you and save my giddy bark.

How I should hate it, Lighthouse tall and
slim,
If you should cut your hair and dim your fire!
My Seventh Wife did that; she doused her
glim,
And dousing it, she damped my soul's
desire—
I took a brick and shaved the rest away,
But still her memory stirs me. . . . Well-
aday!

VIII.

THERE is a freckle just below thine ear
That might have been a theme for Shake-
    speare's art . . .
A fleck of gold out of thy golden heart,
A stain that makes thy stainlessness more
    dear,
Tossed by thy tidal blood as flotsam here
In its warm voyage through every lovely
    part . . .
Hang Shakespeare, Sue! And don't let
    freckles start!
I'd just as lief see optics with a blear.

Your hair's your one best bet. Hold on to
    that.
My Eighth Wife had that silly freckle
    notion . . .
I soaked the poor girl in a vat of lotion
So much that presently she pined away. . . .
She never had been very strong nor fat. . . .
These dear dead women, Sue! Ah, well-
    aday!

"I soaked the poor girl in a vat of lotion"

13

IX.

ALL ardors of the flaming dawn are thine.
Its glamours blended in thy glowing hair!
And sunset winds within thy blowing hair
Have twined and woven all the sunset's
    shine!
And all the quick and kindling heart of
    wine
And heat of wit are in thy flowing hair. . . .
Suzanne, be sure you *keep* that growing
    hair:—
If you turn bald you never can be mine!

MY Ninth Wife used peroxide on her
    bean . . .
She had bad luck; it turned her wig bright
    green . . .
I took a club and chased the girl away,
Although the poor thing pleaded hard to
    stay. . . .
Suzanne, I hope *you'll* never make a scene.
They grieve one later, Sue.   Ah, welladay!

X.

SOME blind and witless boobs, Caloric
    Cutey,
Are moved to scorn red hair, to spoof and
    mock . . .
Not I . . . 'Od'swounds! . . . it biffs me
    with a shock
Electric, overwhelming me with beauty.
My soul (your salamander, Tootsytooty!)
In fancy dwells 'twixt lock and burning
    lock . . .
And had I twenty souls the whole derned
    flock
Were yours, O Flame that nevermore grows
    sooty!

My Tenth Wife bobbed her hair . . . I got
    an axe
And just for that I bobbed the lady's
    head!
Alas! the memory of sweethearts dead
Still from love's current largesse claims a
    tax!
I hope *we* will not part in just that way,
Suzanne . . . But who can tell? Ah, well-
    aday!

"I took a club and chased the girl away"

XI.

MY BLAZING JEWEL! in thee all gems have
    part:
Red garnets and red rubies hot and bold,
Enkindling diamond and mellow gold,
Quick levin flickering at the opal's heart,
And the prismed crystal's fiery-edgèd dart,
All blent to dazzle him that dares be-
    hold. . . .
A Red Head, says the world, will always
    scold . . .
This lowbrowed world! It thinks it's
    Awful Smart!

Ah me! that sad Eleventh Wife of mine!
She nagged me, in a shrill, high, tinny
    tone,
Until I hogtied her with hammock twine
And bound her, talking, to a gramophone,
Within a cell where each jaws each
    alway . . .
These voices of the past! Ah, welladay!

XII.

SUN of my Heaven! Harvest Moon of love!
Bright Planet! Comet! . . . whether earth
    or sky
I scan, your Pink Bean meets my spirit's
    eye,
O peer of flowers beneath and stars above!
O Aphrodite's Crimson-Crested Dove,
I love you as New Englanders love pie!
Vesuvius Girl! your fiery head fling high
And give yon leering Zenith's face a shove!

My Twelfth Wife used to go about with
    twisters
Of kid upon her hair to keep it curley . . .
I pulled it all out by the roots . . . Poor
    girlie!
Her baldness rather shocked her aunts and
    sisters . . .
She died soon after . . . Ah, that's
    woman's way!
They leave us flat so often! Welladay!

" This lowbrowed world "

XIII.

When I approach the chill Lethean river
And stand, all astral gooseflesh, on the
    brim,
Will your Red Head shine for me through
    the dim
Damp shadows where I rub my soul and
    shiver
As I await old Charon's hydro-flivver?
A Lighthouse on the Other Shore? A Glim
Of warmth and courage o'er the waters
    grim?
Will you be mine on Earth and mine
    Forever?

Suzanne, I hope things will not go so
    far . . .
My Thirteenth Wife would say: "Eternity,
My spouse, is not too long for you and me!"
It made me writhe! I painted her with tar
And touched her off and watched her
    blaze away. . . .
How love's old embers burn! Ah, well-
    aday!

XIV.

WHEN I grow older will you be my wife?
Not now, Suzanne . . . in twenty years or
    more.
Unless I change my mind, I'd like you for
A Bonfire in the Autumn of my Life.
But, no! You may be faded then with
    strife
Of living . . . marry another, I implore!
And raise me up your daughter to adore,
Red Haired, with your own candent
    beauty rife.

My Fourteenth Wife had *unresponsive*
    hair,
As drab in tone, inert to touch, as clay;
She wore it in an ugly little knot;
She had a morbid interest in prayer,
Which vexed me so I had to have her
    shot. . . .
She's with the angels now! Ah, welladay!

"As I await old Charon's hydro-flivver"

XV.

SUZANNE, I bring you ornaments of jade,
Dark green to mingle with the shifting
    green
Of your cat's eyes. You are a cat, my
    Queen,
White-toothed and tigerish . . . but I'm
    afraid
Sometimes the part's a trifle overplayed.
Some day, when you decide you'll make a
    scene,
Some one will bend a poker o'er your bean
And you will lead a solemn street parade.

Don't get too temperamental, Susan dear,
With me! You dress the part that fits
    your hair,
But don't scratch, Sue, nor get upon your
    ear,
Nor be too serious with that Feline Stare!
My Fifteenth Wife would kid herself that
    way . . .
But she has left me, Susan! Welladay!

XVI.

AGAINST what background should I paint
    your head? . . .
Relieved upon such paler gold as falls
Through groined and mullioned windows
    on the walls
Of storied minsters, crumbling like their
    dead?
I will not paint it, Kid! Your sort of red,
As full of pep as redhot cannon-balls,
Titians must splash across the frescoed
    halls. . . .
Mine ain't the art for it, when all is said.

My Sixteenth Wife told every one that
    called:
"When I was married my hair was so long
That I could sit on it!" The story palled
In time, and she that told it stole away
Into Oblivion . . . haply I did wrong
To choke her with that hair? Ah, wella-
    day!

"Before you snowed so over all"

XVII.

DANTE for Beatrice sang his solemn story,
Dan for Beersheba all his poems wrote,
Alpha in fair Omega's praises smote
The lyre, and Petrarch jollied little
    Laurie . . .
Suzanne, I'll make you famous, too,
    b'gorry!
Like other Well-Known Couples of great
    note,
Your earnest, honest and industrious Pote
Will cover both himself and you with
    glory!

Alas! my frail Wife Number Seventeen . . .
In memory still I see her dandruff fall!
"I loved you once," I told her, "O, my
    queen!
That was before you snowed so over all
The house . . . now, Human Blizzard,
    blow away!"
She blew. Her memory lingers . . . Well-
    aday!

XVIII.

IF I were blind, my spirit still would see
Thy being break my midnight with its
    glow . . .
If I were lying dead I still would know
A warm difference didst thou pause by me,
So strong the glorious vital heat of thee!
Caloric Kid! you melt the winter's snow. . .
I would sit up and want to be your Beau
Even if drunk, O Incandescent She!

My Eighteenth Wife dropped hairpins by
    the score,
Pitter-patter, everywhere she ambled,
Jingle-jangle, everywhere she rambled,
Sidewalk, table, hammock, chair and
    floor . . .
I drove a dozen in her head in play
One time . . . She took it serious . . .
    Welladay!

XIX.

ALL ardours, prisms, glamours, gems of gold,
All flame of wit and fiery blood of wine
Have blent their brightness in that hair of
    thine!
Worn as thy woven crown, or all unrolled
And blown by amorous winds grown over-
    bold,
It gives the twilight back the morning's
    shine,
And all fresh hearts put tendrils forth to
    twine
Them with thy living glory, fold on fold.

Thy hair! . . . it falls in tides of turbu-
    lence
Across the lyric wonder of thy throat,
In tides that drown my dazzled vision's
    sense . . .
Said Wife Nineteen: "Your sonnets get my
    goat!"
I cried: "Your hair is like drab-coloured
    hay!"
I choked her with it, Sue . . . Ah, well-
    aday!

XX.

SUZANNE, give me a lock of that bright
    hair!
Shear from the burning frame about thy
    face
One vital flame, one strand of living grace,
And it shall warm me until death, I swear!
Trust me, Suzanne, to handle it with care—
I have had made a cute asbestos case:
Over my heart the keepsake shall have
    place,
Sewed in the winter flannels that I wear.

My Twentieth Wife had all too pallid
    lashes,
And her thin eyebrows, too, were almost
    white.
I shaved them off . . . some incidental
    gashes
Made her to moan and murmur all that
    night,
And with the dawn her spirit passed a-
    way . . .
How fragile women are! Ah, welladay!

XXI.

O LOVELY Griddle where my Cakes of Song
Are baked! O Gulf Stream of my ocean
    deep!
O Human Thermos Bottle! will you keep
My love as hot as this our whole lives long?
Or will the slow years moderate the strong
Caloric currents? . . . gradual years that
    creep
To frost Love's tootsies where he lies
    asleep . . .
Shall our fate be that of the common
    throng?

Well, you at least will live in memory;
And that, Suzanne, is more than I can say
Of my Wife Number Twenty-one, for she
Out of my mind has faded quite away.
Too vague to be a ghost! She worshipped
    me,
No doubt . . . but one forgets! Ah, well-
    aday!

XXII.

As THE mad lark rises, drunk with song
    and sun,
When morning bends above the dewy
    meadow,
And his clear call proclaims: "The Day is
    won!"
Over a hurrying rout of driven shadow,
So likewise do I sing, my Sugar-Bun,
When your red bean floats into sight,
    sweet Kiddo!
It fills me full of joy . . . it makes me,
    Hon,
As happy as a Million Dollar Widow!

My Twenty-second Wife wore nightcaps,
    Sue . . .
Frilled things, with cherry-coloured ribbons
    stuck
Upon them. When I pulled one off, as
    luck
Would have it, why the lady's head came
    too!
Anger made me too rough, as anger may,
No doubt. So died our romance! Well-
    aday!

XXIII.

YOU are a Torchlight Rally, Susan! Flare!
I'll be your Given Point, my Torchlight
  Dame . . .
Do you pass by me, crowned with fiery
  fame,
And you will keep me happy sitting there
Unto eternity, to watch your glare!
I am a Bug! I am your Moth for flame!
Pete Pyromania is my middle name—
Gosh-ding it, Sue, I *like* your kind of hair!

Ah, Twenty-three! that fateful number
  cursed
My third-and-twentieth marriage from
  the first!
Scarce were the orange blossoms off her
  when
I found those blossoms had concealed a
  wen . . .
Ah, twenty-three! In my rough, kindly
  way
I played the surgeon, Susan . . . Well-
  aday!

XXIV.

I HAD a dream, and in the dream they said
You were no more, and took me to the
place
Where you lay buried; over your bright
face
Bright grasses grew, and bright flowers
nourishèd
Out of the loveliness of your bright head—
And as I stood there, weeping for a space,
A faint voice murmured, "Susan was the
Ace
Of all those more than ninety wives you
wed!"

The number on your tomb was Ninety-
two!
My Four-and-Twentieth Wife I took in
play
And showed her where her predecessors
lay,
One time . . . Why do I tell you these
things, Sue?
I don't believe in dreams, Sweetheart,
do you?
But still they make one pensive! . . . Well-
aday!

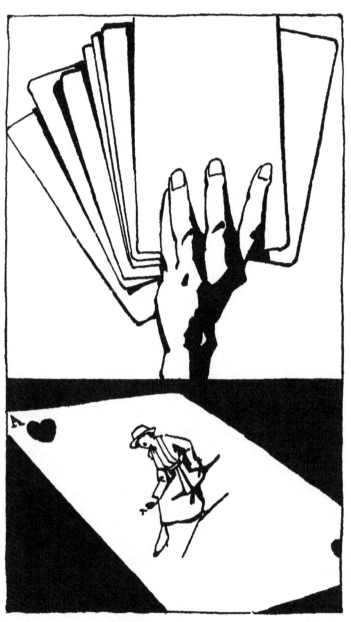

" 'Susan was the Ace' "

XXV.

SINCE first man's eyes unsealèd were in
    sight
One word has been the symbol of his hope;
Wanting that word, the soul itself must
    grope
In a thick speechlessness as blank as night,
Seeking to say itself: That word is "Light!"
Suzanne, were I Hell's darkest misan-
    thrope
And your red head came bobbing up the
    slope,
I'd cry, "Cheer O! Here's Sue! Things
    are all right!"

Old kid, I spoof you frightfully, I know,
But underneath it all . . . you get me,
    Sue?
Wife Twenty-five had hair that turned to
    snow
Because I joshed her just as I josh you . . .
But you, you *like* my playful little way!
Some hearts were broken by it! Welladay!

XXVI.

SUZANNE, my Beard is Blue, whether I
    shave
It close or let it float ambrosial on
The breeze like sprays of lilac cloud at
    dawn . . .
Blue as the tossed and curled and ravelled
    wave,
Reef-combed, that coils about some ocean
    cave
Where the coy smelt creeps to woo the
    flattered prawn . . . .
Sooze, what a poster we would make if
    drawn
Together by some cubist loud and brave!

If drawn together, Sue! The artist, Fate,
Has drawn and scrambled us in just that
    way . . .
Wife Twenty-Six wore on her desert pate
A wig . . . I tied it to an opera chair
One night; and when she rose it dangled
    there
And left her bald and broken. . . Wella-
    day!

"Drawn together by some cubist"

XXVII.

BLUE is my Beard, Suzanne; my Beard is
    Blue!
Blue as the nose that graduate drunkards
    wear . . .
Blue as the tumbled meadows of wide air
Pallas Athene's chariot plunges through. . .
(I don't know why I drag in Pallas, Sue,
Except the name sounds rather flossy
    there) . . .
With my Blue Beard and with your Crim-
    son Hair,
Affinities predestined, Me and You!

Mayhap I've told you why Wife Twenty-
    seven
Left me to mourn and climbed the starry
    way
Up from a thirty-dollar flat to Heaven?—
Suzanne, the woman carelessly turned
    gray!
I gently slew her one sweet Autumn even. . .
These poignant old regrets! Ah, Wella-
    day!

XXVIII.

SPLENDOUR Incarnate! Great Auroral Blaze!
Pillar of Fire, that through my mortal
    night
Still burns to give my groping spirit sight,
I'm gonna bean your Dad one of these days!
"Carrots," I heard him call you, and
    amaze
That such a Ribald Boob, by no means
    bright,
Should be your parent overwhelmed me
    quite.
"Carrots," he called you! Blast his vul-
    gar ways!

Listen, Suzanne: he'd better get a job!
He cannot board with us when we are wed,
That pear-nosed, goat-chinned, fish-
    mouthed, prune-eyed slob!
My Twenty-eighth Wife had a Dad I fed:
They ate and ate until both passed away
Through eating Prussic Acid . . . Well-
    aday!

XXIX.

THY motion fills the eye with minstrelsy,
As if thou wert a Song one could behold. . .
Proud sails of Venice steeped in ruddy gold,
Singing their colour down the charmèd sea,
Move onward clad in music like to thee . . .
As long as you can keep from getting old
I'm for you, Brick-Topped Sue, nor
 shall grow cold,
O Pink-Domed Theme for my Hyperbole!

My Twenty-ninth Wife used to change
 and change
And change the way she wore her hair and
 say:
"Now, *don't* you like it better, Love, this
 way?"
She seemed exhaustless in her hirsute
 range . . .
I scalped her, Susie dear . . . Ah, Well-
 aday!
How sweet old memories are, how rare and
 strange!

XXX.

YOUR mother, turning to me suddenly,
Caught the broad sunset on her triple chin
And nigh her ample and too friendly grin,
Where cheek joins neck in blown obesity,
A faint red whisker was confessed to me.
Suzanne! if *you* should feel a beard begin
Be resolute and to the hilts thrust in
These silvern tweezers that I send to
    thee . . .

And if nor strength nor sleight of art avail,
Oh, still be resolute, Suzanne, and play
The nobler part; a dagger here I lay
Beside the tweezers, Sue . . . My Thir-
    tieth's tale
Deals with a Wart that naught could
    charm away;
A tale so sad, so sad! Ah, Welladay!

"Above the clutching hands of Fate"

XXXI.

WHY do you let Mose Billups call you
    "Sue?"
That rodent-minded, mutt-faced, wolf-
    eared Mose,
That muddy blackhead on Life's pitted
    nose,
That dull negation of the good and true!
Yes, I have heard him call you "Soosie,"
    too!
And once he said you were "a fullblown
    rose" . . .
Good Gawd! to fall for phrases such as
    those
When I write Sonnets such as these to you!

Suzanne, perhaps you don't appreciate
The fact that I, in this immortal rhyme,
Lift you above the clutching hands of
    Fate
And make you bronze to blunt the edge of
    Time!
Some of my earlier wives were blind that
    way . . .
Where are they now? Alas! and Welladay!

XXXII.

WHEN Dian o'er the purple ocean springs
The porpoise spouts in glee, the penguins
    crow,
And all the glad sea lions leap and blow
Their trumpets till the well-known welkin
    rings.
And something kindred in me jumps and
    sings,
Suzanne, when your red bean's supernal
    glow
Flings heavenly light about you as you go
Across the beach in your new bathing
    things.

'Tis more than what you wear, or even
    what
You do not wear, that stirs my lyric blood;
You are my moon, my planet bright and
    hot,
I'm like the wallowing creatures of the
    flood:
The tidal moods of me you mete and sway.
One wife *would* bathe in stockings! Well-
    aday!

"Something kindred in me jumps and sings"

XXXIII.

THE poet blots the end the jester wrote:
For now I drop the dull quip's forced
    pretence,
Forego the perch'd fool's dubious emi-
    nence—
Thy tresses I have sung, that fall and float
Across the lyric wonder of thy throat
In dangerous tides of golden turbulence
Wherein a man might drown him, soul and
    sense,
Is not their beauty worth one honest note?

And thee, thyself, what shall I say of thee?—
Are thy snares strong, and will thy bonds
    endure?
Thou hast the sense, hast thou the soul of
    me?
In subtle webs and silken arts obscure
Thou hast the sense of me, but canst thou
    bind
The scornful pinions of my laughing mind?

XXXIV.

I DID not wish to love thee, for I hate
To have a woman clinging to my soul:
My gods have made it hard to seek their
    goal
Without the burden of that added weight.
Some men there be, triumphant over fate,
Who say they gain more freedom through
    control
Of a binding love that dominates the whole
Of them; I find it hard to abdicate—

Will Love let no man call his soul his own?
Whether I walk in shadow or in sun
My spirit dies unless I walk alone;
I loathe this cant that says two souls grow
    one!
But thou wilt call it infidelity
Unless I share my jealous gods with thee.

XXXV.

STRIP off my mask of laughter from my face
And find it seamed with stark realities:
The eye absorbs the soul of what it sees,
And I stare long at things whose bleaker
    grace
Seldom in woman's warmer realm has
    place—
Thy days are rapt with mortal mysteries;
I dwell among austere philosophies,
Dreaming of life and time and death and
    space,

Old gods resurgent, music visible;
Serene, aloof and chill I love to sit,
Tranced in a thought of heaven and earth
    and hell;
My dreams I hedge about with bitter wit.
Passion I understand, but ask not Faith—
How quick I'd leave thee for some Muse's
    wraith!

XXXVI.

WARNED by a thousand dreams, I took no
    heed,
But failed to fence my soul away from thee;
Mine inner being guessed what thou
    couldst be,
Brooding upon an unacknowledged need—
And now the hush'd thought trembles
    toward a deed:
For sudden beauty bursteth over me
As a great wave fraught with magic of the
    sea,
And I, who was a rock, I seem a reed!

But even a tower were shaken with this
    stress
Of gathered tides unloos'd in love's as-
    sault—
Of gathered tides: more than *thy* loveliness
O'erwhelms and puts my bleak resolves to
    fault:
All women loved before, all loves denied,
Weigh in the surge that batters down my
    pride!

FAMOUS LOVE AFFAIRS

PARIS AND HELEN

PARIS was a pretty gent,
  His lamps were quite hypnotic;
He used the most expensive scent;
  His tastes were . . . well, erotic.

Helen was a timid skirt,
  All she asked was quiet . . .
But, if simps *will* try to flirt,
  Can ladies start a riot?

Now should a frail, or wise, or coy,
  Or innocent of folly,
Scream because some Honey Boy
  Hands her out a jolly?

This Paris had a black mus*tache*,
  I think I ought to mention . . .
Once Helen drooped a blonde eyelash:
  It drooped *without intention* . . .

But *he* pretended for to think
   She drooped it of election:—
"Ah, ha!" he cried, "you wink! you wink!
   Then buss me, Greek confection!"

Which took the lady by surprise,
   And striving to expound it,
She winked again, with both her eyes—
   And bussed him too, confound it!

She slapped him then, and told the guy,
   "Villian, you unhand me!"
And he looked grieved and made reply,
   "You misunderstand me!"

"O, prithee, do not think," she cried,
   "That I kiss gent'men chronic!"
"I know—trust me"—returned the Snide,
   "Your buss was but Platonic!"

With smooth remarks like that he laid
   Her natural suspicion . . .
It was a devil's part he played!
   Nor did he feel contrition.

"Paris was a pretty gent"

He'd take her to see shows as hot
    As if they had been peppered;
She'd blush . . . *he* never changed a spot:
    He was a Moral Leopard!

And oft, with blushes that would make
    Her brow and cheek and chin burn,
She'd listen while this Subtile Snake
    Lisped her the Pomes of Swinburne.

Now Helen's husband saw them kiss . . .
    A sandy man, well gingered . . .
And after several years of this,
    Says he, "I think I'm injured!"

This husband was a man of strength . . .
    Few characters were finer . . .
And when she left her home at length,
    Traced her to Asia Minor.

Bill Homer's told the rest, I think . . .
    Fights and fires and phrases . . .
What started out with Helen's wink
    Wound up with Hell 'n' blazes!

The moral of the tale is this:
  That mayhem, death and arson
Have followed many a thoughtless kiss
  Not sanctioned by a parson!

KING COPHETUA AND THE
BEGGAR MAID

COPHETUA was a merry King,
  And slightly sentimental;
His morals were (if anything)
  What some call "Oriental."

Zenelophon, the Beggar Goil,
  Was innocent and careful;
She had been reared to Honest Toil
  By parents poor and prayerful,

For Papa peddled lemonade
  While Mamma laundered laundry,
And she had been a solder maid
  Within a muzzle foundry;

But, oh! the foreman of the staff
  Had tried to Make Advances . . .
The Villain used to smirk and chaff
  And ask her out to dances! . . .

And so she quit the Hellish Place
    And went salvationarming,
A careful smile upon her face
    So innocent and charming.

While begging in a Beer Saloon
    Right opposite the palace
She saw the King one afternoon
    Drink chalice after chalice—

(He dallied daily with the Jug,
    He hit the pipe and gambled,
He introduced the bunny-hug
    As round his realm he rambled)—

Eftsoons the Monarch, reeling by
    Imperially laden,
Remarked, iniquitous and sly,
    "Pray, buss me, Beggar Maiden!"

"Not I!" she cried, "I'd rather go
    Right back to making muzzles
Than kiss a King that roisters so
    And gambles, flirts and guzzles!"

"Drink chalice after chalice"

69

The Regal Cut-up, in a mood
   Majestically reckless,
Then offered her a samite snood,
   A duchy and a necklace.

"Oh, keep your Royal Gauds," she said,
   "And buss your legal spouses!
I won't kiss none until I'm wed,
   Especial if they're souses!"

With that he laid his sceptre down
   Beneath her footsy-wootsies—
"Oh, wed me, and I'll fling muh crown
   Before them pretty tootsies!"

"O King!" says she, "you *have* some
    queens!"
   Says he, "They're soon beheaded!"
That day his headsman reaped their beans,
   The next the King was wedded.

And Mrs. King Cophetua made
   All parties quit their vices,
And Papa's private lemonade
   Soon rose to fancy prices,

And Mamma laundered for the King
As happy as a linnet—
Oh, Virtue always wins, I sing,
If Wisdom's mingled in it!

TRISTRAM AND ISOLT

I.

Sir Tristram was a Bear, in listed field
Or lady's bower, Champeen with sword or
    song;
All that life's traffic could be made to yield
Trist took; he'd tell some Sweet Thing,
    "You belong!"
And with that word he'd cop her from the
    throng.
Boudoir or tourney, tea or dancing green,
He never kept them waiting very long;
Nor Foe nor Frail had really turned his bean
Until he lamped King Mark of Cornwall's
    sprightly Queen.

II.

Mark was a Pill. His Little Dame had
    Class . . .
One of those Unions that neglect to Une . . .
She was a Saint! He was a Hound! Alas,
73

That such a Peach should marry such a
    Prune!
Why did she stick? Who knows the in-
    ward tune
To which these women march? We know,
    at least,
Mark had a Wad, and bought her gowns
    and shoon . . . .
Also, one eats or one is soon deceased. . . .
Mayhap it was a case of Booty and the
    Beast!

III.

TRISTRAM rode by her palace on a day
When some young angel leaned from
    Paradise
And loved the earth and laughed and made
    it May;
And Izzy saw his lovely purple eyes—
Not the young angel's: Tristram's; other-
    wise
She might have flagged the angel for her
    Beau
Instead of Tristram. Ah! what tears and
    sighs
Were saved if women never looked below
The angels . . . yet, no doubt, at times
    they'd find it slow.

"Rode by her palace on a day"

75

IV.

As SHE gave him the rapt Once Over, he
Felt all his bounding pulses pause, then fill
With love as tidal creeks flood from the
    sea. . . .
Sir Tristram, if you get me, got Some
    Thrill. . . .
One jump and he was at her window-sill,
The Sudden Cuss! "Divinity!" he said,
"Newly descended from th' Olympian
    Hill,
I'm yourn! Say, are you single? Are you
    wed?
If so, where is your Spouse?—I'll go and
    chop his head!"

V.

"I'M NOT Olympian, sir," she said, "but
    only
Of this hick realm the melancholy Queen.
You love me, Stranger? Thanks! I get
    so lonely!
As for your kindly offer to unbean
My liege lord, 'Ataboy! I *loathe* a Scene,

As all Nice Women should, but *this* is Fate!
No girl can dodge her destiny, I ween. . .
Or do I dream? Pinch me!—Ouch!
  Don't ! I'd *hate*
To have you get some Horrid Notion in
    your pate!

VI.

"I KNOW you'll think me Unconvention-
    al!"—
"What are Conventions 'twixt Affini-
    ties?"—
"I always thought love was more grad-
    ual!"—
"Let Temperate Zones grow warmer by
    degrees,
But why should we Equators think of
    these?"—
"Why does your mustache taste that funny
    way?"—
"Something the barber does."—"Stop
    him!"—"Say *please !*"—
"Please, then—and *could* you murder
    Mark *to-day ?*"—
"I'll cut his throat 'mid the sweet twi-
    light's tender gray!"—

VII.

AH, PRETTY prattle, innocent and artless!
Sweet interchange as when lute answers
    lute!
These cooing doves! what Fiend could be
    so heartless
As wish to make their happy murmurs mute?
What Fiend but Mark!   That wicked, sly
    old brute,
Whenever his fair wife would kiss a
    stranger,
Would scowl at her and even stamp his boot,
Or read her lectures on A Young Wife's
    Danger—
When Home is Hell what wonder if Love
    proves a Ranger!

VIII.

THE Spoilsport crept behind them as they
    kissed
And slammed the window down across
    their necks,
Nor any guardian spirit grabbed his wrist,
And in one instant both of them were
    Wrecks!

The sad tale's Moral goes for either sex:
Don't spoon beneath a giddy guillotine
If any one's about whom it may vex—
Make love quite out of windows or quite in
If you aspire to keep a chest below your
    chin.

IX.

AND so they died, in Cornwall by the sea,
Where tides asthmatic ever wheeze and
    snortle,
And the damp tin miners going home to tea
Still hear sometimes old Mark's com-
    placent chortle
As his lean ghost by a ghostly window-
    portal
Slams phantom sashes down and gloats
    and gloats. . . .
And so they died, and so they are im-
    mortal,
And in Elysian meadows feel their oats
Forever! Death can never get true lovers'
    goats!

OTHELLO AND DESDEMONA

OTHELLO's heart was weathered oak,
 And so was his complexion;
He was, no doubt, the Biggest Smoke
 In Venice's collection.

He'd served Venezia's Duke, his liege,
 From Cyprus to Bologna,
And 'twixt a battle and a siege
 Eloped with Desdemona.

An F. F. V., this artless gal—
 First Family of Venice—
Who played along the Grand Canal
 Splash, squash and water tennis.

She was quite blonde.   Her father said:
 "By Heaven, this is tragic!
That Dinge could not have turned her
    head
 Unless he'd pulled some magic!"

"I pulled no stuff that wasn't right—
  Us Tans and us Gamboges,"
Othello bragged, "can act as white
  As any pale-faced Doges!"

Fate loosed upon this twain a man
  Of guile and gab, Iago,
More subtle, slick and sinful than
  A Buyer from Chicago.

Insinuation was his game.
  He used to say: "Old Varnish,
You better watch your Little Dame!—
  The brightest love will tarnish."

Or else: "I could unfold a tale!
  But no . . . you'd think me boorish . . .
You keep your eye upon that Frail . . .
  You watch her, Swart-and-Moorish!"

No open charge, you understand—
  He *named* no wild young fellas—
But *hinted* things behind his hand . . .
  It made Othello jealous.

And so one night he killed his wife . . .
  Then learned he'd been mistaken . . .
"Well, well," he murmured, "such is life!"
  It left him rather shaken . . .

Her friends and kinfolks gathered round,
  And said: "Old Black-and-Tarry,
You certainly have played the hound!"
  Othello said: "I'm sorry!

"Alas! the pillows piled above
  The one I should 'a' cherished!"
And saying so he opened of
  Himself with prayer, and perished.

The moral is: Don't go and wed
  Some shine like this Othello,
But let your parents pick a man
  Without a streak of yellow.

ANTONY AND CLEOPATRA

CLEOPATRA Ptolemy's fad
  Was playing Aphrodite;
From Hind to Italy she had
  The name of being flighty;

She'd often send a bid to say:
  "On Friday is my wedding!
Come . . . and stop till Saturday
  And witness the beheading."

Scarce a beau could keep his bean
  Safe from axe or sickle . . . .
Egypt smiled and said, "Our Queen
  Is just a trifle fickle!"

Antony, the lucky wight,
  Was a Roman winner,
Ladies used to scheme and fight
  To get the gink for dinner;

"'I need some drammer'"

85

Old medallions show him where
  He prances through the Corso
With his glad, pomatumed hair
  And his noble torso.

Waking one day sad with debt
  And blue with *katzenjammer*
He mused, "I've not seen Egypt yet. . . .
  I'll go; I need some drammer!"

He found the Queen attending, bored,
  A morning tiger party,
A farewell to a former lord . . .
  The guests were doing hearty. . . .

She *saw* him . . . *he* saw her . . . the
    rest,
  For neither was ascetic,
Was Robert Chambers at his best—
  Some folks are *so* magnetic!

Says she, "You stay in Egypt, kid,
  And can them Latin minxes—
I'll deed to you a pyramid
  And half a dozen Sphinxes!"

Says he, "You keep your trinkets, ma'am,
    I am not mercenary . . .
I do not give a diadam
    For aught but you, my fairy!"

Though Fate is skulking in the wings,
    Our Strong-Arm Tony clasps her . . .
Oh! let's be brief with tragic things . . .
    Fate enters next, and asps her!

CLEOPATRA ON MRS. MARC ANTONY

YOUR representative has seen the Serpent
   of Old Nilus
About the Antony Affair; and never has
   my stylus

Been called upon before to sketch a char-
   acter so charming . . .
Although, at times, Her Majesty has moods
   that are alarming . . . .

"I Live my Own Life," Cleopatra said,
   "and my intent is
To persevere in that respect; I'll follow
   what my bent is!

"You say that Fulvia's suing me for eighty
   thousand dollars?
A Woman who can't Hold her Husband
   always peeves and hollers!

"But what a *bourgeois* thing to do! How
    common! And how Roman!
By Isis, kid, a thoroughbred would put a
    price on no man!"

The queen received me on the roof directly
    after dinner;
She's looking . . . well, she is *some* queen!
    Perhaps a trifle thinner

Than when she met Jule Cæsar on that
    gink's Egyptian mission . . .
The time he told his wife she'd ought to
    be above suspicion. . . .

She gave me coffee in a cup carved from a
    single ruby;
As she was pouring it a slave, a thick
    thumb-handed booby,

Spilled some upon her royal neck, which
    rather riled our queenlet—
She swung a jewelled scimitar and nicked
    his Nubian beanlet. . . .

The Nile, below us, squirmed and flashed
    with phosphorescent fishes.
And now and then a crocodile, content and
    unambitious,

Would root against the palace steps and
    scratch his back and bellow,
Or some lorn hippopotamus would warble
    for his fellow . . .

And now and then, as we conversed, the
    queen. in merry mood O!
Would kick a courtier from the roof to give
    her pets their food O!

"I *loathe* Conventions," said the queen.
    "My Soul cannot be harried
With Trivial Things!   I will not be Victor-
    ian, Trammelled, Married!

"I *gotta* be *Myself*, old kid, and if as such
    I break up
Some Home monogamous, what then?   I
    cannot help my make-up!

"Soul-mates are Soul-mates! Get me,
    kid? I always had a leaning
Towards Freedom, kid! You otta Give
    your Love a Higher Meaning!

"You got that down? I *must* express myself!
    —And you might mention
That to my mind there's nothing as *wicked*
    as Convention!"

"Serpent," I said, "another point perhaps
    you'd care to answer:
Fulvia has spread the word, from Capricorn
    to Cancer,

"That while you have the will to be a
    reg'lar Moral Leper
She has you faded, frail to frail, for pul-
    chritude and pepper—

"She says, in short, your Work is Coarse,
    your tricks are out of kilter,
And that you'd not 'a' trapped her Mark
    but that you used a philtre."

"Did she say that?" Miss Ptolemy rose,
    ferocious as a Bulgar,
Then calmed herself and murmured low:
    "My Gawd! How crude and vulgar!

"You paint 'em blue, or chalk 'em white,
    or rub 'em with erasers,
Their Commonplaceness will stick out on
    all these Commonplacers!

"This Mrs. Marcus Antony is really quite
    pathetic;
It's Personality that wins, not Poses or
    Cosmetic—

"But why should I get sore at her? I'll not
    descend to bandy
Words with such a low-browed skirt . . .
    nor send her poisoned candy."

And yet it seemed to me the queen, be-
    neath her calm external,
Was somewhat stung: for as I left I heard
    a noise infernal:

Next day I learned that she had loosed a
    large man eating tiger . . .
A pet particular of hers brought northward
    from the Niger . . .

Among her royal servants who, in rushing
    from the palace,
Were met by waiting crocodiles. I think
    she harbours malice . . . .

She took a dozen female slaves and named
    each "Mrs. Tony,"
And fed them to the ibises, and did it all-
    aloney!

Sometimes our little queen is calm, sweet-
    natured, soft and gentle;
And then again she's something else . . .
    She calls it "Temper'mental."

"In rushing from the palace"

QUEEN ELIZABETH INTERVIEWED

YOUR Representative has seen Miss Queen
    Elizabeth,
And talked with her of Marriage, Men
    and Mary Stuart's death.
'Twas one of great Eliza's Spacious Days;
    she said her say
At length, with point and heat—as always
    on a Spacious Day.

"That little red-head Stuart Minx," began
    the noble Queen,
"The best day's work they ever did was
    amputate her bean!
The blank-blanked little Green Eyed Cat!
    By Priam and by Hek,
These royal hands of mine they ached to
    nick that woman's neck!
She wasn't Moral, kid! And as Walt
    Raleigh used to say,
Do what you d——d well please, but do it
    in a Moral Way!"

She paused and drank a quart of ale, and
    then Her Majesty—
Without abating jot or tipple of her
    dignity—
Leaned from her gilded throne and shied
    the dripping tankard at
A lacy bishop's *embonpoint*, and knocked
    the varlet flat.
Encouraged by her playful mood, the
    somewhat jovial tone
That mingled so with majesty, as words
    wed to a lyre,
A Chancellor pushed up to her a thick
    north country squire:
"I knight you, Dub," the Queen remarked,
    and smashed his collar bone.
The Queen is full of grace and charm and
    quaint, unstudied ways,
Especially on what are known as Liza's
    Spacious Days.
"'Od's blood!" the Queen went on, "I've
    heard some blank-blanked whey-faced
    ginks
Have said I should have pardoned her;—
    but Mary was my Jinx!
By gad!" . . . she banged the sceptre down
    and all the court turned pale . . .

"The wight that mentions her is lucky if he
goes to gaol!
That dame was always getting wed! She'd
dress up like a horse
And flag a man and marry him! I think
there's Something Coarse
In any blank-blanked Princess that has
Marriage on her bean—
To hell with Men! I've stayed Refined . . .
I am the Virgin Queen!
The Earl of Essex used to say when he
came here and dined,
'I gotta hand it to Your Grace! Your
Grace is so Refined!'"

Your Representative, though trepidant,
found heart to say:
"Your regal dad viewed Marriage in a
rather different way."

"Yes, Dad," she said, "was crude and
coarse, the time he reigned in, ruder—
I've got to raise the average for the whole
d——d House of Tudor!"

She broke a splinter from a stool that stood
the throne beneath
And quite reflectively she picked her lovely
yellow teeth . . .

Those teeth of which her Poets sing: *Oh,
    ivory and gold!*
*They shine like morning in her court!   Ah,
    wondrous to behold* . . .
And as she picked the Regal Teeth, Lord
    Burleigh ambled by,
And, still reflectively, she flicked the
    splinter in his eye.

"In former times the kings cut up like
    butchers, bards or tanners,
But I have always tried to be a Model in
    my Manners.
The Earl of Leicester used to say when he
    dropped in to dinner,
'My Liege's daintiness alone would make
    My Liege a Winner!'
And also, please to state for me, I Pat-
    ronize the Arts—
This whole damned palace here is cluttered
    up with Men of Parts.
As Walter Raleigh used to say . . . when
    he came in to tea . . .
'I gotta hand it to Your Grace for Cultured
    Ways,' says he."

Your Representative made haste to say—
    what is but true—
"Of all the Great I've interviewed, ne'er
    did I interview
A personage, Your Majesty, who had a
    thing on you!"
"Don't flatter now!" she said, and smiled:
    and as she smiled a sort
Of smiling sigh went whispering around
    the nervous court—
For something of anxiety shows in the
    courtier's gaze
When Great Elizabeth begins one of her
    Spacious Days.

Beaumont and Fletcher trotted up, and
    kneeling by her throne,
These Siamese Twins of Drama chanted in
    a dulcet tone
Their latest song in praise of her, the
    Great Elizabeth . . .
Her moods are changeable . . . she rose:
    "'Od's blood! " she cried: "'Od's
    Death!"

And snatching off her coronet, when Beau-
mont's mouth oped wide,
With more than female force she jammed
the jewelled knob inside . . .
And catching up his weapon from a drows-
ing halberdier
She poked it part in Fletcher's eye and
partly in his ear . . .
"Ye bean-fed rogues," she said, "avaunt!
Heraus!   How didst thou dare
In thy blank-blank-ed song to say thy
Queen had golden hair?
Hath it not been proclaimed to all, in
village, thorpe and town,
That on last Michaelmas the Queen's long
yellow hair turned brown?"

I thought it best to take my leave.   "Your
Majesty," I said,
"Some monarchs would have had these
beasts well boiled in oil instead."
Whereon Sir Francis Walsingham said to
Her Majesty:
"They got to hand it to Your Grace for
kindly leniency!"

ROMEO AND JULIET

Pop Montague's old brain was wried
  Through all its convolutions
With constant thoughts of Homicide
  And kindred institutions.

White-haired Giuseppi Capulet,
  Although he liked his daughter,
The pert, precocious Juliet,
  Was fonder still of slaughter.

Young Romeo was just designed
  To play Italian opera:
A looker, with a tenor mind—
  A *perfect* star for Wopera.

Each cutthroat father kept at hand,
  In their respective houses,
A low-browed, cloaked, romantic band
  Of swordsmen, thugs and souses.

When ennui made Giuseppi sad
  He'd go a-Montagueing;
Pop Montague's perticler fad
  Was Capulet-pursuing.

How could young lovers dodge their doom,
  With all these complications?
They gravitated to the tomb
  To join their near relations.

Their bloody story I might trace—
  How loved they but to rue it—
At length if I but had the face,
  But Shakespeare beat me to it.

(They're Shakespeare's corpses—let him
    hop
  About his morgue and sort 'em—
I'll start where he came to a stop
  And pull a brief post-mortem.

Will for the dagger and the kiss,
  The poison and the quarrels,
But my preoccupation is,
  Far more than Will's, with morals.)

So when the feud had run its course
  And slain its scores and dozens
The ancient cutthroats got remorse—
  And gave it to their cousins.

Quoth Capulet: "We're here to-day—
  But where are we to-morrow?"
Pop Montague would often say:
  "I feel a sort of sorrow!"

Remorse soon heightened to regret;
  They signed a bond one Monday—
Old Montague and Capulet—
  To slay no man on Sunday!

Their hearts grew softer with the years.
  Their mood grew kind and pensive—
They mused, one morning, bathed in tears,
  "Some days, crime seems offensive!"

Salt globules furrowed each lank cheek,
  They thought of son and daughter,
And vowed that more than once a week
  They'd not indulge in slaughter.

Upon their own reform they'd gloat,
  In consciousness of virtue,
And murmur as they cut a throat:
  "I'm sorry if I hurt you!"

Thus Montague and Capulet,
  They took to heart the lesson,
And so the death of Juliet
  In some ways proved a blessin'.

And this reform of which I speak
  Made them far less dejected—
They stuck to murder once a week
  And died loved and respected!

PETRARCH AND LAURA

A TASTE Francesco Petrarch had
   For dialects, and leeks, and verses,
Though Laura was his best-known fad . . .
   But Laura loved her Husband (Curses!)

Through twenty long and tragic years
   That burned Francesco's soul like acid—
(He melted several Alps with tears)—
   Laura remained at home . . . quite
     placid.

She loved her Husband, Laura did:
   Please fix that vital fact securely.
When Petrarch called her "Heavenly kid!"
   She'd blush and drop her eyes demurely.

Not that he ever saw her more
   Than once or twice in any quarter . . .
Food took his time, dialects, and war . . .
   For months she'd think he'd stopped it,
     sorter.

'Twas A. D. 1331
He studied Greek (historians say so)
And sang, "She warms me like the sun!"
And boned up P. Ovidius Naso.

I think 'twas 1339
  He learned the speech of Kurds and
    Coptics,
And, flushed with love and Tuscan wine,
  Penned three canzoni to her optics.

In 1328 he wrote,
  "I cannot live a year without her!"
In 1346 I note
  A similar remark about her.

From thirteen-twenty-nine to thirt-
  Een-hundred-forty-eight she never
(Though he septennial tried to flirt)
  Smiled once upon his bold endeavour.

She loved her Husband.   And her Home.
  She loved her Babes.   She had eleven.
While Petrarch wrote pome after pome—
  Sonnets three-hundred-twenty-seven!

"'I cannot live a year without her'"

And all white-toothed Italia smiled,
  Commenting pleasantly upon it—
"Dear Laura has *another* child!"
  "Hast lamped Petrarco's latest sonnet?"

She perished: (1348).
  "Alas," he sighed, "I never kissed her!"
His sonnets, onward from that date,
  Lead one to think he somehow missed
  her . . .

She died, and Earth held little more:
  Vain all its garlic, gauds and laughter!
He pined. In 1374,
  Not thirty years, he followed after.

By Venus, in those Southern climes,
  How quick and reckless is love's fashion!
In colder latitudes and times
  We dwell and learn to curb our passion.

HERO AND LEANDER

LEANDER in the Dardanelles
    Had rather race a dolphing
Than idle with the other swells
    Or dance or go a-golfing.

In church at Abydos one day,
    At a revival service,
He saw young Hero, and the way
    He lamped her made her nervous.

And after that, along the coast
    He would do fancy swimmin'
Graceful enough to charm the most
    Fastidious of women;

When she'd go bathing, dawn or dark,
    About her bathing station
He'd frolic like a friendly shark,
    Or like a coy cetacean.

"He would do fancy swimmin'"

What maiden's heart could long resist
　　Such sweet and shy devotion?
Full often, when he dived, she kissed
　　And patted his pet ocean!

Leander, on flirtation bent,
　　Across the straits was floating
One morning when her mother went
　　To chaperon her boating:—

"Oh, mother, may I marry him?"—
　　"Oh, no, my darling daughter!
When young Leander goes to swim
　　Don't you go near the water!"

Alas! that maids should disobey,
　　Whom parents trust and bless so!
Girls will be girls . . . in Hero's day
　　They were not any less so.

Next time she heard him in the sea
　　Snort like a loving grampus,
Says she, "Swim over after tea—
　　It's dark. and none can lamp us!"

And after that, to light her love,
  She used to show a candle . . .
It grew to the dimensions of
  A reg'lar seashore scandal . . .

But finally Neptune, Triton, or
  Some ordinary porpoise,
Caught him a mile or two from shore
  And served a *habeas corpus.*

The night was cold . . . the sea was
    damp . . .
  Alas, for him and Hero!
The moral is: *Don't risk a cramp*
  When the water's down to zero.

"Adam was a handsome lad"

ADAM AND EVE

Adam was a handsome lad,
    Innocent and merry;
Garden parties were his fad,
    And he was honest, very.

Eve was rather artless; she
    Was also quite vivacious;
She plucked her raiment from a tree
    Elæocarpaceous.

Satan was a City Man,
    Wicked, dark-complected . . .
He paled as only villains can
    When Eve his love rejected. . . .

Satan was a chap who used
    To sin with conscious pride, O!
He drank, he swore, he introduced
    The Boa Constrictor Glide, O!

119

When she turned the fellow down,
  Though with rage he trembled,
Satan smoothed away a frown,
  Smiled at her, dissembled . . . .

But he'd think of it and curse
  While he drank or gambled;
Thoughts of dark revenge he'd nurse
  As round the world he rambled.

He muttered, "This is not the end;
  You'll repent it, Madam!" . . .
But he posed as Family Friend
  When she wedded Adam.

Years went by, and still he came
  Once a week to dinner;
His outward mood was bland and tame,
  But evil was his inner.

Quite informal he'd drop in,
  Dine and help do dishes . . .
Who could think he planned a sin?
  Who'd believe him vicious?

But every time he wiped a plate
   Or helped poor Adam buttle
He'd sneer inside and meditate
   Something smooth and subtle.

At last he gained in Adam's house
   A plausible position;
At last he lulled, in Adam's spouse,
   Her natural suspicion.

He rooned 'em . . . then he gave a hiss,
   A glide and boa-constricted . . .
Details are told in Genesis . . .
   I think they were evicted.

LANCELOT AND GUINEVERE

KING ARTHUR was a steady king,
   Who loathed light talk or skittish,
Respectable as anything,
   Strong 'eaded, blond and British.

His Queen beside him on the throne,
   So golding 'aired and tidy,
Would tip the beam at fourteen stone,
   And every ounce a lydy.

Sir Lancelot was 'andsome, quite,
   The women all adored him—
He tried to bear it like a knight,
   But being worshipped bored him.

His big, bright shield was curved and bent
   And more tub-shaped than normal;
He'd frequent halt a tournament
   And bathe, all stern and formal.

The knights, they might 'ave bashed 'im
   then
While 'e was coldly scrubbing,
But they were British gentlemen
   Respectful of his tubbing.

'E loved 'is Queen, and she confessed
   'Is love reciprocated;
It grieved 'em both . . . they did their
   best
But *could* not feel elated.

"My word," Sir Lancelot would sigh,
   "What rotten form to love 'er!"
And then 'e'd gloom and say good-by . . .
   Return . . . and gloom . . . and hover.

The Queen would call 'erself a fraud—
   She *hated* loving, madly!—
"It's using Harthur bad . . . Oh, Gawd!"
   The Queen would mutter sadly.

"To think," says he, "I'd act the same
   As any foreign bounder!"
And moaning with a sense of shame
   He'd put his arm around 'er.

She'd kiss him, while repentant tears
    Fell salt on his proboscis . . .
For seventeen long mournful years
    They nobly bore their crosses . . .

'E moralized, grew thin, austere,
    And groaned, awake or sleeping;
But she grew bloated, Guinevere,
    With self-reproach and weeping.

When Honest Arthur learned the fac's
    It shocked him so completely
The court opined they'd get the axe . . .
    Instead, he took it sweetly . . .

King Arthur says, "Me for the tomb,
    Where no disgrace can grab us!"
The Queen crept sobbing from the room
    And went and was an Abbuss.

And Lancelot, he moaned and said,
    "I 'ope no one will guy 'er!
For me, I'll shave my blooming 'ead
    And go and be a friar."

The moral is: Observe your bent,
  Your own traits mark and measure—
If one has not the temperament
  Philandering isn't pleasure.

SOLOMON AND BALKIS

From Beersheba up to Dan
Another such a caravan
Dazed Palestine had never seen
As that which bore Sabea's queen
Out of the fain and flaming South
To slake her yearning spirit's drouth
    At wisdom's pools, with Solomon.

With gifts of scented sandal-wood
And labdanum and cassia-bud,
With spicy spoils of Araby
And camel-loads of ivory
And heavy cloths that glanced and shone
With pearl inwrought and beryl-stone
    She came, a bold Sabean girl.

And did she find him sad, or gay?
Perchance his palace breathed that day
With psalters sounding solemnly—
Or cymbals' merrier minstrelsy—

Perchance the wearied monarch heard
Some loose-tongued prophet's meddling
   word;—
    None knows, no one—but Solomon!

She looked—with eyes wherein were blent
All ardours of the Orient;
She spake—all magics of the South
Were compassed in the witch's mouth;—
He thought the scarlet lips of her
More precious than En Gedi's myrrh,
    The lips of that Sabean girl.

By many an amorous sun caressed,
From lifted brow to amber breast
She gleamed in vivid loveliness—
And lithe as any leopardess—
And verily, one blames thee not
If thine own proverbs were forgot,
    O Solomon, wise Solomon!

She danced for him, and surely she
Learnt dancing from some moonlit sea
Where elfin vapours swirled and swayed
While the wild pipes of witchcraft played

Such clutching music 't would impel
A prophet's self to dance to hell—
  So spun the light Sabean girl.

He swore her laughter had the lilt
Of chiming waters that are spilt
In sprays of spurted melody
From founts of carven porphyry,
And in the billowy turbulence
Of her dusk hair drowned soul and sense—
  Dark tides and deep, O Solomon!

Perchance unto her day belongs
His poem called the Song of Songs,
Each little lyric interval
Timed to her pulse's rise and fall;—
Or when he cried out wearily
That all things end in vanity
  Did he mean that Sabean girl?

The bright barbaric opulence,
The sun-kist Temple, Kedar's tents,—
How many a careless caravan
From Beersheba up to Dan
Within these forty centuries
Has flung their dust to many a breeze,
  With dust that was King Solomon!

But still the lesson holds as true,
O King! as when she lessoned you:
That very wise men are not wise
Until they read in folly's eyes
The wisdom that escapes the school,
That bids the sage revise his rules
  By light of some Sabean girl!

DIDO AND ÆNEAS

ÆNEAS was a cattle boy,
    And his career was checkered;
Bull after bull, by roaring Troy,
    He threw, and copped the record.

Troy down—and Helen tripping back,
    Remarried by the rector,
To Greece—Æneas took his pack
    And beat it west, by Hector!

He took a ship, and *mal de mer*
    From Colonel Neptune's ocean
Crept up and shook his steamer chair
    And filled him with emotion.

A storm came up—(and other things
    Too intimate to write on:
When Triton spouts, both clowns and king
    Will spout right back at Triton.)

"Too intimate to write on"

And in the straiter seas his craw,
   If anything, was iller—
He lost his spirit when he saw
   Charybdis teasing Scyller.

And so he climbed the raging seas,
   Green hummock after hummock,
And got to Carthage, ill at ease
   And qualmish in the stomach.

Queen Dido met him at the wharf
   And poured him out a potion;
Says she: "You takes this bumper orf
   And you forgets the ocean!"

He drank. He calmed. And then says he:
   "Old dear, I like that tunic!"—
He doted on good clothes, and she
   Was portly, pink and Punic.

She blushed, and then said with a smile:
   "Although I am Phœnician,
I always try to dress in style,"
   Says he: "You're more than Grecian!"

Thus, like so many other gents,
   Who're pleasant when they're grateful,
He fed her up with compliments,
   Not knowing they are fateful.

For all he meant was gratitude,
   To pay her for her potion,
But she construed his attitude
   To indicate devotion.

He only tried to be polite,
   Which   charmed her . . . more's the
       pity! . . .
And she'd assure him he was quite,
   Quite welcome to her city.

Well, well, . . . his words went to her
       bean . . . .
   She led him to a cavern
And mixed him drinks . . . the poor, dear
       Queen!
   Folks sneered: "She runs a tavern!"

He sailed one day . . . the royal frail
   Had even picked the parson! . . .
It is a truly tragic tale;
   She killed herself with arson.

Do not as serious construe,
 Fair maids, each small attention,
Or there may come a fate to you
 Too turrible to mention!

HARLEQUIN AND COLUMBINE

WHEN the soul of the year through its body
  of earth
Burst forth in a bloom as of fire,
And the butterflies rose in a rainbow riot
  of mirth
To flutter and burn and take wing and
  aspire,
To her garden our Columbine came . . .
She was light as her laughter, and bright
  as blown flame—
Flower, woman and music, and all these the
  same.

Harlequin
Was a wind of the Spring that came out of
  the dawn;
He was air, he was whim, he was fancy and
  mirth,
And his feet on the earth
Were as fleet as the feet of a faun.

He was fickle as glimmers of starlight that
    shine
On the waves of the rivers of dream; he
    was tricky as wine;
He was pagan as Pan;
A dancer, a lover, a liar, a wit,
A poet, a satyr, an imp with the face of a
    man;
And his heart was unstable as wings are
    that lift
Where the dragonflies drift,
His heart was as wings that turn, dartle
    and flit,
And his loves were as swift.

And into her garden he came like a spiral
    of wind that beats down in a shower
Red flower and white flower . . .
And their hearts were as swift as the doves
    in their flight,
Their love was the love of the youth of the
    world . . .
They mingled, they danced, they were shod
    with delight,
They were sandalled with joy . . . .
She was lifted and whirled,

She was flung, she was swirled, she was
    driven along
By this carnival wind that had torn her
    away
From the coronal bloom on the brow of the
    May
In a whorl as of rapture . . . their danc-
    ing was visible Song!

His moods were as light as the airs of the
    dawn;
He loved for an hour, and was gone . . .
What matter if flower and red flower
Were flung down in a shower,
And blossom, and blossoms, were trodden
    and dead?
It was only a wind that had danced with a
    flower,
When all's done and said!

THE END

CPSIA information can be obtained
at www.ICGtesting.com
Printed in the USA
BVOW04s1600040917

493918BV00014B/119/P